antoinette portis
Hey, Water!

NEAL PORTER BOOKS
HOLIDAY HOUSE /NEW YORK

Thanks to the United States Geological Survey for their help.

Neal Porter Books

Text and illustrations copyright © 2019 by Antoinette Portis
All Rights Reserved
HOLIDAY HOUSE is registered in the U.S. Patent and Trademark Office.
Printed and bound in January 2019 at Worzalla, Stevens Point, WI, United States of America.
The artwork for this book was made with brush and sumi ink. Color was added digitally.
www.holidayhouse.com
First Edition

10 9 8 7 6 5 4 3 2 1

Library of Congress Cataloging-in-Publication Data

Names: Portis, Antoinette, author, illustrator.
Title: Hey, water! / Antoinette Portis.
Description: First edition. | New York : Neal Porter Books, Holiday House, [2018]
Identifiers: LCCN 2018009006 | ISBN 9780823441556 (hardcover)
Subjects: LCSH: Water—Juvenile literature.
Classification: LCC GB662.3 .P688 2018 | DDC 553.7—dc23 LC record available
at https://lccn.loc.gov/2018009006

Hey, water! I know you!
You're all around.

faucet

sprinkler

You spray up

and down.

shower

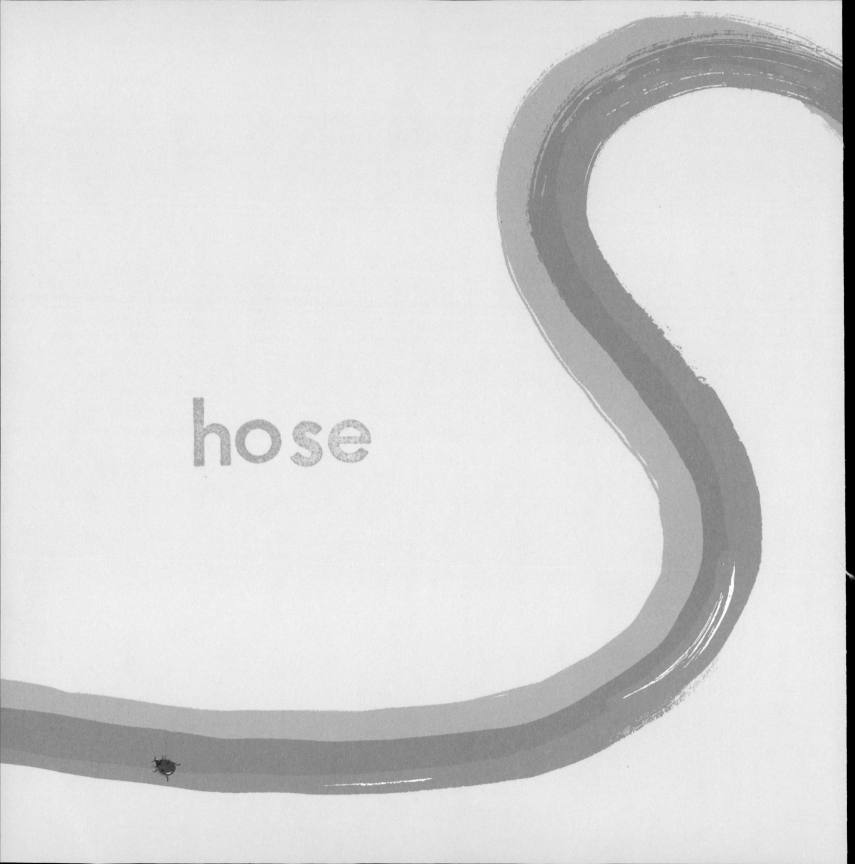

hose

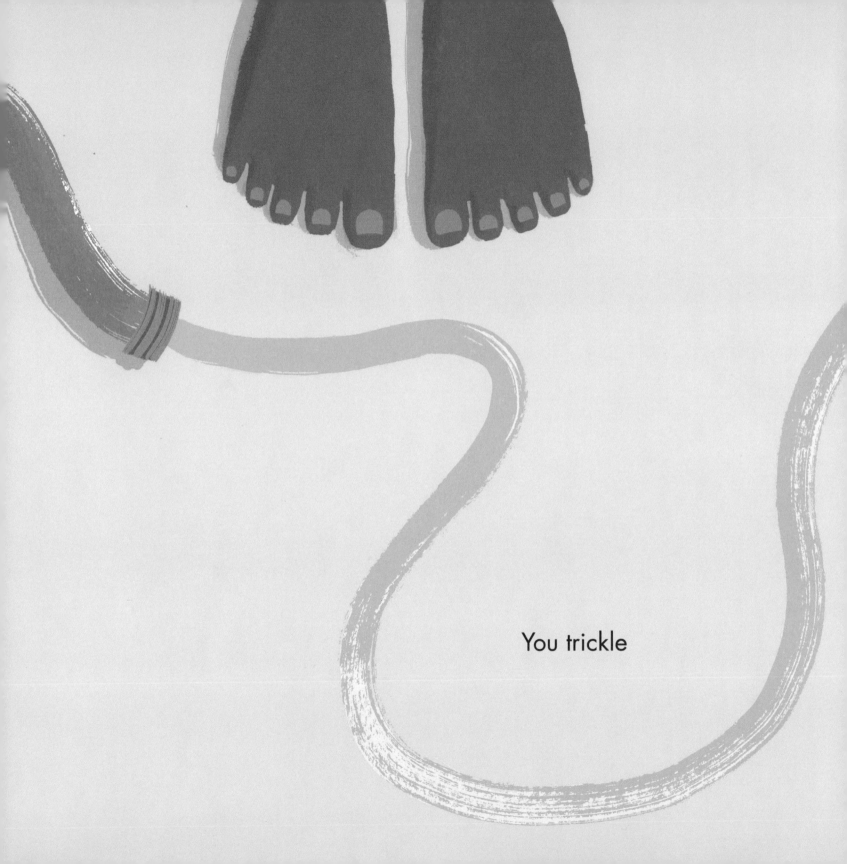

You trickle

and gurgle

stream

river

and rush toward the sea.

You cover most of the earth—
salty, surging, and mysterious.

ocean

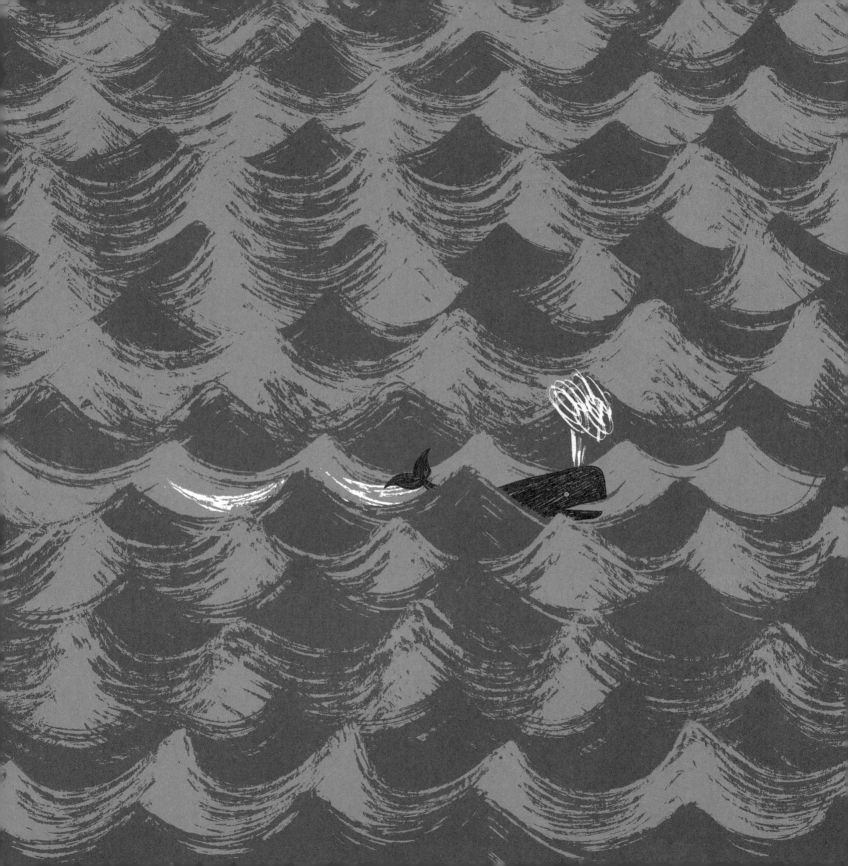

Sometimes you lie, quiet and calm,

lake

so we can splash and play
and yell in you.

pool

I stomp in you and
scatter droplets everywhere.

In the morning, you wink at me from blades of grass.

dewdrop

Sometimes you slide down my cheek without a sound.

tear

rain

Sometimes you roar and pour.

Water, even when you try to fool me, I know you.

You blast and huff.

You whistle and puff.

steam

You hide in the air and drift.

cloud

You drift in the air and hide

fog

the world.

Sometimes you freeze hard as a rock—

ice cube

iceberg

a rock that floats,

or a rock we can skate on.

rink

Sometimes you freeze soft as a feather

snow

and fancier than lace.

But water, I know it's you!

snowflakes

You're hiding in this funny guy, and you're hiding in me, too!

snowman   Zoe

Water, you're a part of every living thing.

When I'm thirsty, there you are.

bathtub

Hey, water, thank you!

water forms

liquid

We know water as a liquid, flowing from a faucet to fill a glass, rushing by in rivers on their way to the sea, and providing a home for millions of creatures and plants. But water is not just amazing because it's necessary for life on earth. Water can take many forms beyond the liquid we drink every day.

Clouds and fog don't look like liquids, but they are made of tiny droplets of water, so tiny they can float in the air. When the drops clump together and get too heavy to float, they fall from clouds as rain.

solid

When water is cooled way down to 32 degrees F (0 degrees C) it freezes into a solid. Solid water appears as tiny crystalline snowflakes, ice cubes clinking in your glass, or icebergs the size of city blocks floating in the seas of Antarctica. Water in its solid state can even fall from the sky in the form of hail as big as tennis balls and dent the roofs of cars!

gas

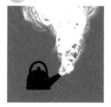

Not gas! Steam is actually tiny drops of hot water.

Gas. This is what water vapor looks like—nothing! It's invisible! It's in the air all around you.

When water is heated, it turns into a gas called water vapor. In this form, water is invisible. Water vapor is in the air all around us, but we can't see it. We think of steam as vapor (gas), but actually it's not. Steam is a mist made of tiny droplets of hot water suspended in the air. That's what we see shooting out of the spout of a kettle or hovering over a bowl of soup. Water turns into vapor at room temperature, too, though this happens so slowly we can't see it. This is how rain puddles on the sidewalk gradually disappear—the sun's warmth evaporates the liquid into gas.

the water cycle

condensation
Cold air causes water vapor to turn back into liquid droplets.

precipitation
Water falls to the ground as liquid or solid.

evaporation
The sun's heat turns liquid into vapor that rises up into the air.

collection
Water runs downhill and collects in rivers and lakes, as well as seeps down into the ground.

This cycle has repeated over and over again for millions of years.

conserving water

We are lucky that in most places in our country, we can turn on a faucet and get clean water to drink. There are many homes in the world where this is not true. Some people need to walk miles every day to get the water they need to drink, wash, cook, and grow food.

Though the same amount of water has been on the earth for millions of years, almost all the water on earth is in oceans. Seawater is salty, so we can't drink it or grow plants with it. Freshwater, found in lakes, rivers, springs, or underground—the water we drink and use in daily life—is only 3% of the water in the world, and 2% of *that* water is frozen in glaciers and the polar ice caps, so we can't use it.

In many parts of the world, we are consuming our freshwater faster than it falls to earth as rain or snow, while a warming climate is drying up lakes and rivers around the world. We need to use our freshwater supply carefully, especially in times of drought. If we don't, then all living things won't have the water needed for survival.

If you want to find out more about the wonder that is water, here are books to explore:

Bright, Michael. *From Raindrop to Tap*. New York: Source to Resource. Crabtree Publishing Co., 2017. Print.

Green, Jen. *How the Water Cycle Works*. Our Earth. New York: PowerKids Press, 2008. Print.

Flanagan, Alice K. *Water*. Simply Science. Minneapolis: Compass Point Books, 2001. Print.

Stewart, Melissa. *Water*. National Geographic Kids. Washington, DC: National Geographic, 2014. Print.

For fun, hands-on water experiments for young children, check out this workbook:

Bittinger, Gayle. Illustrated by Mohrmann, Gary. *Exploring Water and the Ocean*. Everett, WA: Warren Publishing House, 1993. Print.